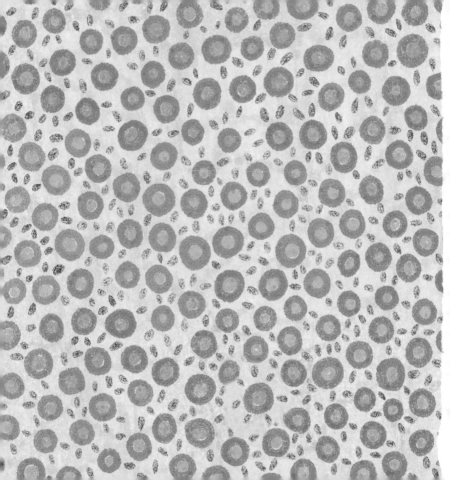

thanks
to you

thanks
to you

illustrated by mary engelbreit

written by patrick regan

**Andrews McMeel
Publishing**

Kansas City

www.maryengelbreit.com

and Mary Engelbreit are registered trademarks of Mary Engelbreit Enterprises, Inc.

03 04 05 06 07 LPP 10 9 8 7 6 5 4 3 2 1

Design by Stephanie R. Farley and Delsie Chambon

ISBN: 0-7407-3150-5

Your friendship means
so much to me
I don't know where to start.
All I can do is
thank you
From the bottom
of my heart.

Thanks to you
my day is brighter,
And my spirits
have been raised.

Your kind words and
thoughtful gestures
Always leave me
quite amazed.

Thanks to you
the world seems calmer.
Your wise counsel
helps so much.

CUP OF
KINDNESS

When it comes to
putting folks at ease,
You've got the
magic touch.

Thanks to you
I know I'm not alone
When clouds of
worry hover.

You stand with me
to face the storms
When others
run for cover.

And when we're back
on solid ground
You add snap to my stride.

Good times
are even better
When I have you
by my side.

So when I count
my blessings
I count your
friendship first.

My gratitude
can't be subdued
To hold it in I'd
burst!

Thanks

for listening,

Thanks

for caring,

Thanks
for comforting
and sharing

Thanks

for keeping confidences
And forgiving
past offenses

Thanks for calling
when I'm blue
Thanks for *whew!*
just being you.

I'll always be so grateful
For the things
you say and do.

My world's become
a better place
And it's all been
thanks
to you!